Brainwashed From Birth

Brainwashed From Birth

How to Liberate Yourself from the Family Narcissist

Linda K. Castor, LCPC

Published by Get to the Point of It Press

Paperback ISBN: 979-8-9905326-0-1

Brainwashed From Birth

Linda K. Castor, LCPC

Get to the Point
of It Press

TABLE OF CONTENTS

PART FOUR
Self-Healing Strategies and Deprogramming Techniques

PART FIVE
Beyond Grey Rock and New Protective Techniques

CONCLUSION

ACKNOWLEDGMENTS

With immense appreciation, I thank my clients for teaching me valuable lessons throughout their struggles. I couldn't have written this book without you. We all need each other's music to direct this symphony of life.

I am indebted to three special friends, Barbara Bunjevac, Miriam Stokes, and George Hinkle, who held my hand during my grieving process. Thank you for your patience and kindness.

To my writing coach, Charlotte Rains Dixon, and our gifted Zoom writing group, especially Kim Poovey, for their valuable advice, and all my other cherished friends. Thank you for supporting my writing journey.

I extend a huge thank you to my family for your encouragement, especially my daughter and fellow author, Jessica Souther, who inspired me to publish this.

To my readers and listeners, I am honored to share my experience with you. May you feel my love, gratitude and support. Advancing our knowledge to empower ourselves and touch the lives of others is one of the greatest gifts we can offer. Please share your gifts with us.

Thank you to Valerie Williamson for her editing prowess and author Gini Chin, talented cover artist and formatting extraordinaire, for your expertise and generous support.

Last but never least, to my husband, favorite cheerleader, and best friend of twenty-seven years, William Castor. I am grateful I found a patient man who helped me tame my once out-of-control soul.

WHY I WROTE THIS BOOK

Now that I'm enjoying a life free of narcissistic abuse, why am I writing a book about it? I believe the more we share our stories and experiences, the more we connect our wisdom. If a book like this had been published years ago, I would have benefitted from learning how to decipher the heartbreaking and chilling truths about a narcissist's mind and engage with other family members who lost their way inside a hostage-like environment.

In this book, I address deprogramming, a subject that's fascinated me since childhood. No wonder I was mesmerized while watching a television special back in 1980 about a man who knew how to deprogram family members who succumbed to cults. I discuss the steps I took to deprogram myself.

Realistically, some of us don't have the luxury of abruptly leaving the narcissistic relationship. Beyond grey rock, a method of acting unresponsive to a person's toxic behavior, I developed techniques that insulated me from my narcissistic mother. I was shocked they worked so well to protect my psyche while I engaged with other family members.

In my case, I needed my dad. I tuned out his brainwashed pleas for me to make peace with my mother and patiently listened to why he felt "caught in the middle." Under my mother's reign, my dad and I were not allowed to have a close connection. We learned to communicate with our eyes when I visited their house as she leeched onto me and monopolized our conversations.

I'm grateful my dad and I found our way back to one another. We meet for lunch and have great conversations. I get to know him now. He's 91, so our time is fleeting yet precious.

By extending myself to my dad, he rescued me, too. His love is like a healing salve on my heart wound. The more he validates me, the more I feel my mind and soul return to a normal I have never known. I already forgave him for relinquishing his mind to an insane woman and following through with her orders to throw me across the room when I didn't obey one of her ridiculous rules. Together, we peeled back our layers of conditioning.

I may have lost one parent, but I gained another.

This book is meant to offer you solutions as you firm up any decision to go "no-contact" while cultivating immense compassion within yourself, your conditioned loved ones, and maybe even the tortured soul we call a narcissist.

You can learn how to navigate around narcissists, plan your cutoff, and never become a target again.

It is the way to free yourself.

INTRODUCTION

Love, grief, and pain over losing my mother to narcissism ignited my desire to understand what happened to her—and to me.

I was brainwashed from birth to believe my mother was normal and I was not. She convinced me she had the right to rule and plan my life because she was my mother. I was to obey her no matter how cruel the punishment or unreasonable her demands were.

I was livid and hurt after realizing what had happened to me, and I was determined to understand everything about narcissists. I watched YouTube videos about their callous manipulation and cruelty. I even went into crusade mode and wanted to save as many as possible from these dreadful people.

Then I noticed a disturbing psychological trend within myself and on social media. Narcissist was becoming a buzzword, a blanket diagnosis, thrown out there to cover anyone who demonstrated emotional detachment or self-serving behaviors. No doubt labeling was done out of fear; better to identify someone as a narcissist instead of falling prey to them all over again.

The problem with blanket labeling is that it overlooks the fact that not everyone is a narcissist. Anxious people can resemble narcissists when they are forthcoming, bossy, or controlling because they feel out of control. Some people express explosive anxiety, and this most definitely triggers abuse survivors.

The growing intensity of division in our world encourages more hateful rhetoric. The "us versus them" mentality fuels the falsehood that we are separate from one another. If everyone is not on the same page of understanding, then a power struggle is born. It is an unsustainable, repetitious pattern. Underserved people eventually revolt, and madness enters the minds of those who only seek power in the absence of love.

Love is the answer and is the calling of this book: to inspire survivors turned thrivers to wake up from the deep sleep of our programming and understand our truth, that we are one, connected, and can expand love within ourselves.

This book is a vital healing guide for anyone who has just awakened to the truth of being raised by a narcissist and is now contemplating the harsh reality that they are disposable, like a piece of trash, in the eyes of this parent. The term supply is prevalent in today's social media. It accurately explains how narcissists see and need us. To them, we are a toy to be played with and then abandoned without a care.

I'm here to reassure you that you're not alone. You can overcome the narcissist's hijacking of your identity and reclaim your true sense of self.

I spent months reading and commenting on some of the

most heartbreaking, gut-wrenching stories I've ever seen on Reddit. I wrote this book for you: the girl who felt estranged and discarded by her parents or the boy who could never measure up to his unruly father. Anyone who wants to learn how to reprogram themselves can use this universal guide from a fellow traveler who has already walked on this road to recovery.

You might feel like parts of you are scattered everywhere in tiny pieces, but you're not broken. We are meant to survive this ordeal and not be like the narcissist. I'm passionate about sharing what I've learned, and I look forward to guiding you toward your continued freedom.

If the person in your life who wounded you was a sibling, caregiver, or extended family member, you can still learn valuable techniques. I'm humbled and grateful to teach my strategies.

Once you heal, please spread the love. I'll be cheering you on.

PART I

My Story

HOW I AWAKENED TO THE TRUTH

There's a loss coming. And I don't want to feel it.
But I can no longer ignore it.
I have to google the question: Why do narcissists refuse to talk through or resolve misunderstandings with family members?

~LKC

I was a truth-teller as a child, and this infuriated my mother. I knew she was controlling and influenced my dad, but I didn't realize how much her behavior would affect me later on.

When I rebelled, she made my life more difficult, often inciting abuse by my father. The part of me that wanted to get through childhood without losing my mind eventually succumbed to her daily doses of untruths and distorted parent modeling. I unknowingly shamed myself in front of grade school peers with grandiose notions I learned from her, and I was highly vulnerable to teasing and an easy target for their amusement.

One day, I reached my tolerance level and told her, "No!"

I knew doing this would risk physical harm, but I was tired of pretending, self-sabotaging, and feeling depressed. I understand now why I depleted myself: If I'm less than her, then her order and hierarchy are restored. If her order and hierarchy are restored, I'm safe for now.

My parents provided me with numerous growth opportunities, and I'm grateful for positive influences, like education and art—two of my mother's favorite subjects for endless pontification.

As an only child, our family of three experienced darker times of addiction and abuse, and I spent years attempting to make her happy in a futile attempt to restore family integrity. After failing multiple times in this solo endeavor, I realized nothing would prevent her from escalating into more tirades.

Despite being brainwashed, I knew something was wrong with my mother. I just thought she was a miserable, crabby, bossy woman.

By the time I acknowledged she had classic narcissistic character traits, I was already a well-established mental health therapist. Unfortunately, I overlooked the crucial fact that I had incorporated her narcissistic traits, which greatly benefited her while crippling my judgment.

Feeling wronged and victimized, I was determined to outsmart her. All my training couldn't prepare me for how she skillfully manipulated me. Dare I say it, I thought I could cure her of narcissism.

If only I had researched more about narcissism to jolt me back into reality, I could have saved myself time and grief. Grief. That's what I was avoiding. I didn't realize it, but I was already in the shock and denial stages.

Not ready to give up, I foolishly marched down a path

that almost sacrificed my sanity to the point of no return. I thought my love would bring her back. It was like a dream opportunity come true. What child doesn't want her mother to be normal, decent, courteous, and someone she could proudly introduce to others?

Then, something amazing happened. As she challenged my boundaries, creative strategies popped into my mind, and I used them. They worked on her, or at least I thought they did, and my mother softened a bit. She toned down her bullying and created an atmosphere of what I perceived as acceptance. My yearning to feel loved by her was now coming to fruition.

But the truth came hurling at me like a dodgeball in the face. The person I was attempting to save stomped on all the hard work I did to repair the relationship. She had to create chaos again, which was a devastating miscalculation on my part. What I didn't know at the time was that I had collected enough information to find effective ways to tolerate her bad behavior.

After that, whenever I called my mother, she abruptly switched from kind, warm, sugary behavior, telling me everything my inner child longed to hear, to answering her landline in a seething, terse, haughty, spit-nails-through-the-phone tone, "What do you *want*?"

At first, I thought this was dementia. But my mother showed she was fully capable of love bombing my precious daughter, the "golden child" in her eyes, which meant I had just graduated to a scapegoat role in this dysfunctional extended family. Like a tidal wave slamming me into the sand, she repeatedly and viciously shut me down and pushed me out to sea.

Coming to terms with the reality you've been brainwashed from birth is quite revelatory, shocking, numbing, and depressing. This means everything you once thought was true, all the things they said, were most likely done because they wanted to control and manipulate you. All the sweet love notes in birthday cards, all the encouragements, and then suddenly an abrasive move on their part, and you become lower than the dust under their shoes.

Shortly after these bizarre hot and cold interactions with her, I searched online for answers.

Who knew the perfect storm, my miracle awakening would occur with one Google search?

Why do narcissists refuse to talk through or resolve misunderstandings with family members?

The chilling answer: *They couldn't give a flying flip about your feelings or problems.* I felt a thickness in my throat and read on. *Because they love to stir up conflict and make it your fault.*

And then, the oh my God moment. It's real. It's true. To her, I am just a chess piece to be toyed with, and now I've just been flicked off the board without a care.

The shock and devastation set in fairly quickly. Tremendous grief radiated throughout my overwhelmed body. The heaviness in my chest was excruciating. I began tapping on the meridian points using the Emotional Freedom Technique I had used for years with clients. I guided my breathing as I replayed childhood scenes that validated the heart-wrenching truth about my life:

My mother had always been a narcissist.

THE ROLLERCOASTER OF SHAME

Am I a bad person?" I asked my husband while relaxing on our comfy couch during an evening of watching TV. I had been in no-contact with my mother for about six months, meaning I cut off all communication except for a hand-painted watercolor birthday card I sent. And I was still hurting. I hadn't yet recovered from years under the mind-bending, soul-altering influence of the cult of one.

The flood of traumatic memories and my brain's attempt to sort them out was overwhelming.

Fortunately, I was not reliving them. But my brain didn't know the difference. Anxiety rose up and toyed with me, just as it did long ago.

My mother used to denigrate my character on phone calls with extended family members. I remember listening at the top of the stairs at night when she'd complain to my dad about their unruly child. I was convinced she persuaded every family member that I was a terrible kid, ungrateful to the core, and unworthy of her love. I thought they all had joined her cult of one. At the time, I felt immense shame because "a mother is right," and I must be a horrible kid if she had to complain to others about me.

She brainwashed and wounded me so deeply that I never questioned the cruelty of it all.

Where was love? I wondered.
What did I learn about love?
Am I a bad person?

Such nauseating questions sent uncomfortable waves throughout my body.

My husband reached over and gently took my hand.

"No, of course not. You're a wonderful person and one of the kindest people I know."

I observed the sadness in his eyes, focusing on mine while reassuring me I wasn't crazy. Throughout our twenty-three-year marriage, his compassion has been my greatest blessing. Tears of gratitude dripped onto the cushions.

"Good. Thank you. I feel better." Oh, my God. What a relief. I'm not an awful person.

Finding little relief from my melancholy, I decided to write my mother a letter from my heart, one that would convey that I didn't hate her. She's eighty-six now, I thought. What if she suddenly died, still thinking I would someday actually dance on her grave?

I can still remember the moment she accused me of doing that as a teenager, and it haunted me.

I also didn't want to wait two months until the dreaded Mother's Day—when everything and anything eventually goes wrong. I felt I had healed on multiple levels and was ready to express my gratitude for her and focus on the good things she has done for me. I carefully crafted the words in this letter for over a month, and it energetically felt honest when completed. I handwrote it and sent it off.

A week passed, and I heard nothing. I'm nothing to her. What a fool. I just put myself in a spiraling funk for sending it and opened myself up for more grief, pain, and rejection.

Her inaction plummeted me into smallness, and my torso felt heavy, crushing my lungs as I breathed. It felt like her silence and inaction were slowly killing me. I imagined her saying, "What now?" as she opened my delicate, sweet, precious love letter to her.

Of course, this revelation occurred in the middle of the grocery store, and it took everything I had to get out of there before I blubbered a flood of tears all over myself. I made it home and started unloading bags on the counter.

"Are you okay?" my husband asked, gingerly peeking in from the other room.

I shook my head while looking down. "No. No, I'm not."

I told him how degraded I felt for writing and sending that letter.

My husband's reassurance was all I needed. His kind words melted my heart and calmed my frenzied mind. He offered a perspective I had not considered. Shame had given me a gift: an invitation to feel humility and humanity.

My husband's response exemplified this truth: "You honored yourself by intending to send love. You proved you have integrity."

Words can be healing. Beautifully crafted words, like the ones he spoke, had the power to shift me to a higher level of thinking and heal me in a way I hadn't felt before.

Processing shame with a loved one or trusted therapist can turn everything around. The right person will say something that transforms your state of being. It's incredible how that happens.

RELEASING YOUR FEELINGS AND THE BALL OF ANGER

There is no right or wrong way to grieve the loss of your relationship with your narcissistic parent. One of my clients abruptly chose no-contact. She cried for a year. Grieving helped her with the final cutoff after she revisited her parent one more time and decided she was ready for her "boundary of done."

When I finally allowed my brain to accept the truth about my mother, I was unprepared for the degree of overwhelming emotions and daily runaway thoughts. It made sense; I had endured a lifetime of indoctrination. How was I supposed to wrap my head around that?

Here's what I learned:

There will be unexpected intensity and quiet contemplation. The grief stages of denial, anger, bargaining, depression, and acceptance go back and forth in no particular order. You may feel like you're in a whirlwind of controlled chaos. But you can find respite in mantras that calm you, such as "letting go and trusting the flow."

Release your feelings instead of frantically trying to suppress uncomfortable emotions that arise once you grasp the reality that a narcissistic parent raised you. If you ignore your feelings, your body will alert you with strange and uncomfortable symptoms, like feeling as if a brick is stuck in your stomach for days. There is no need to suffer from physical manifestations clearly related to your emotional state. In the Self-Healing Strategies section of this book, I share ways you can release them safely and effectively.

However you decide to do this, please don't do it alone. As I've said before, find a support person, preferably a trauma therapist who understands narcissism, while implementing the principles and exercises in this book. You are worth the money it costs to see one.

When you are ready to bravely allow your feelings to grow as big as they need to, the good news is that *even your most uncomfortable emotions will generate a positive outcome,* and you will be rewarded with a gift.

For example, we receive *greater clarity* when we allow our anger to move through and dissipate.

Conversely, when we feel invalidated, we tend to hold on to anger like an invisible, tangible ball, especially if wrongdoers don't sincerely apologize for their misdeeds. And we know narcissists don't ask for forgiveness—they genuinely forget they caused us harm at all. You will learn why they have poor memories later in the book. When anger is the only evidence proving this person hurt us, we'll grip that ball tighter to justify the existence of our pain and say, "See what you did to me? Look how angry I am because of you!"

Letting go of anger before we're ready often backfires. *Be true to your process*, and don't let anyone try to spare you from your feelings. Invalidation creates resentment, and these spiraling thoughts can enslave us within our self-imposed victim loop. It's natural to slide into a victim mentality. We learned it from the narcissist who raised us. Whenever I notice this behavior in myself, I say as a reminder, "You're not a victim." Since I've been doing that, my attitude has shifted, and that "shame ball" is gone. I'm grateful every time I catch myself going into that mode.

When we embrace anger, the hidden gift is strength, energy, and motivation. Knowing this, I was eager to process my rage. With a flat foot, I kicked a brick building and beat the crap out of my beanbag with a Nerf bat. That felt amazing, but I remained furious with the parent who rejected me. I wondered if I would ever be able to release all the anger inside. I wanted to find out.

PART TWO

Definitions and Concepts

THE DIFFERENCE BETWEEN VICTIM AND TARGET

It's difficult to click through reels or shorts these days without finding advice or information about narcissism. I encourage you to watch videos and read articles to learn as much as you can. I credit both lay and professional people for enlightening me.

I learned the most valuable information from Dr. Samuel Vaknin, whose teachings are unique and vital for our greater understanding because he was diagnosed as a malignant narcissist. I weave his message throughout this book and describe his concepts in a more digestible form for trauma survivors in my chapter, An Inside Look into a Narcissist's Mind.*

Instead of regurgitating definitions you can easily find online, I chose specific terms to help you integrate the information I present in the book. The more facts you know, the wiser you'll be to resist temptations delivered by narcissists, whose brains direct them to get what they need from you, regardless of what it does to you, your family, or your

...

*You can learn more from him at https://vaknin-talks.com.

mental health.

First, it's essential you understand the dynamics and differences between victims and targets.

Victims are people *who have already been subjected to* emotional, physical, or sexual abuse by a narcissist. This abuse can take many forms, including gaslighting, name-calling, threats, and intimidation. Victims of narcissistic abuse often feel isolated, worthless, and helpless.

Targets are those *who are being groomed or manipulated* by narcissists. This grooming process can take months or even years, and it is designed to make targets feel unique and essential. Narcissists will often shower targeted people with compliments and gifts and make promises of a future together. Regardless of the method for hooking targets, narcissists will reveal their true demeanor and eventually become controlling, manipulative, and abusive.

Narcissists test to see if their targets have been brainwashed enough to follow along with their plan. They often prey on vulnerable and easy-to-manipulate people, especially if they believe the targets can provide them with something they want, such as money, power, or status.

Shell-shocked by this confusing behavior, demoralized targets will attempt to help or fix the problem. This is a narcissist's dream come true. However, well-informed targets will abruptly exit the situation and refuse to put up with their circus show.

NARCISSISTIC CHARACTERISTICS VS. NPD

Before you read any further, remember that you are the hero of your story. Learning about narcissism may feel intense, but I want you to know that you can handle this. You've survived, you're aware, and now you're planning to bid farewell and climb over that fence to freedom. This book is designed to give you a leg up so you can land safely on the other side.

Narcissism is on a spectrum. At times, we all exhibit traits of selfishness, aggression, and insensitivity.

Individuals with *narcissistic characteristics* may display entitled behavior. However, this can change over time as they learn that the feelings and thoughts they experience are not inherent to their true nature. With a therapist's support, they can successfully curb and eventually eliminate these ingrained behaviors.

I extinguished my traits and now enjoy insights that chip away at old patterns. Whenever I experience this, my mood improves, and my self-compassion flourishes.

Narcissistic Personality Disorder, or NPD, is a mental illness that is difficult to treat because people with NPD may or may not realize these traits are present, are proud of who they are, and see no reason to change.

Symptoms cause significant distress and vary with each person, but classic behaviors are grandiosity, sensitivity to criticism, and lack of empathy.

Do not attempt to manipulate or be reckless with people who have NPD. They will:

- Target you for victimization because they need the companionship of another victim.
- Justify victimizing you as doing you a favor.
- Replace you. They cannot distinguish the value between you and a bowl of noodles.
- Groom you to feel special and then discard you like trash.
- Not honor their agreements.
- Never forgive you for offering help or advice and feel humiliated if you do.
- Find a way to exploit your weaknesses because they believe they know everything.
- Strive to eradicate you.
- Accuse you of being a narcissist.

There are successful methods I use to deal with narcissists that I touch upon in future chapters, but toying with them is not one. Understanding this distinction is clearly valuable to preserve your mental health.

Your goal is to go no-contact as soon as possible. Narcissists have dependent personalities, so even if they push you away, they will attempt to lure you back into their dysfunctional world. We need to be the ones who break free from narcissistic relationships.

As you process this information, what thoughts or revelations occur to you?

COGNITIVE DISSONANCE, TRAUMA BONDING, AND STOCKHOLM SYNDROME

Understanding the relationship between trauma bonding and cognitive dissonance will become very important when you decide to connect with other family members who have been brainwashed.

Cognitive dissonance occurs when a person has conflicting thoughts that cause emotional discomfort. For example, even though my dad knew I was a good daughter, when my mother pressured him to gang up on me, he would take her side and scold me, as she did. He experienced cognitive dissonance, the mental conflict incurred when hurting me (what he didn't want) versus championing my mother (which he felt strangely obligated to do). His actions were inconsistent with what he believed, and later, he felt tremendous guilt. He then needed to rationalize reasons for his decisions to relieve his guilt.

You can observe the pained look on people's faces when they are in this mode. They are aware of feeling psychological distress but believe they are helpless to do anything about it. Narcissists, who are always playing games, have the upper hand and further confuse their victims.

Trauma bonding is a coping mechanism that occurs when an abused person develops a strong emotional attachment to an abuser. There is an imbalance of power and unpredictability. Intense emotions, such as loyalty, love, and fear, develop for the abuser in response to the trauma, and this can be physical, emotional, or sexual. This attachment is reinforced in a cycle as the abuser shows kindness and then reverts back to soul-shattering tactics.

Because narcissists are dependent beings, they foster dependence in their target or victim. They create a distorted picture as they attempt to mold another person into a victim.

I experienced *cognitive dissonance within trauma bonding* after realizing my mother had NPD. I was still attached to her due to years of learning emotional dependency. This inner conflict is why I believe it's unrealistic to tell someone to "just cut off the narcissist." We need time to wrap our heads around this new awareness and sort out our feelings. It is possible to plan your cutoff without causing further harm to yourself.

At one point, *trauma bonding created cognitive dissonance within me* when I questioned why I kept returning to visit my mother, as no matter what I did, she remained cruel and hostile toward me. I knew I deserved better, but I didn't honor that.

There is a term coined after a bank robbery occurred in Sweden in 1973. *Stockholm Syndrome* is when a captive prisoner feels an affinity for the kidnapper. The hostages developed an emotional attachment to their captors despite fearing for their lives. In comparison, a trauma bond is not necessarily life-threatening, but it can be in some cases.

Those of us who grew up with a narcissistic parent

sometimes feel as adults our development was stunted. We were trained to focus our energy on a person who needed attention, not ourselves. We had to overcome feeling criticized, judged, and unloved. Many grow up feeling "not good enough."

What helped me was knowing that I wasn't a weak child; I was human and regressed into a state of dependency to survive the ordeal. Learning this helped me release shame, knowing it wasn't my fault that I gave up so much for her and felt insecure and codependent in adulthood.

Recognizing if you are in a trauma bond is crucial for your well-being. It's not your fault you made excuses for their horrible behavior. You were trained to believe their false promises to change and didn't question when they attempted to separate and completely isolate you from loved ones.

I had heard of love bombing before but didn't realize it was one of the stages of trauma bonding!

When you're in it, you don't see it. Let me tell you, it doesn't matter how intelligent you are, they are cunning with this tactic, even after you've cut them off.

Love bombing is when the narcissist acts kind and thoughtful and appears to have changed into a decent and humane person. But it's a ploy. My mother tricked me into believing she wanted me back in her life because she valued me. She also values ice cream. Narcissists cannot conceptualize the difference.

When my mother's sister died, my cousin called to tell me the sad news. I then reported the death in our family to my dad when he answered his cell phone. He asked me to do him a favor.

Uh-oh, I thought. Here it comes.

"I think it would be best if you called your mother on the landline to tell her."

Ugh. Narcissists are like Forrest Gump's box of chocolates: you never know what you're going to get. I didn't want to call her, and here I was, giving in to a flying monkey. (For anyone who hasn't heard the term flying monkey in relation to narcissistic families, it refers to an enabler or one of the Wicked Witch's monkeys from the Wizard of Oz who were trained to obey her.) I didn't want to disappoint my dad either, so I rationalized. It was her sister, after all. Plus, I knew how to get off the phone quickly. I dialed the house phone.

Of course, my mom was delighted to receive the call and get attention. She was having what I call a "good hair day," so I knew our conversation would at least be tame, with no yelling or chastising.

But then, she did it. She manipulated a love-bombing request in the most pitiful, sheepish tone.

"Since you called your dad on his cell phone, it would be nice if you rang the house phone and all three of us could talk."

Right. I see what you're doing, I thought.

Knowing her memory is poor, I agreed that's what I'd do.

Other trauma-bonding tactics narcissists use are striving to appear trustworthy to gain your confidence, criticizing you to the point where you blame yourself (even if you've done nothing wrong), and manipulating you so they can defend their behavior.

You can sever a trauma bond. Continue to educate yourself about unhealthy relationship patterns. Just like the phone call with my mom, one of the things I always have to remember is whatever comes out of her mouth is false, even though I want to believe her. It's a gut-wrenching exchange, which is another reason why going no-contact is the only solution. And I'm not that gullible little girl anymore.

What parts of my story seem familiar to you?

THE HIDDEN GIFTS OF YOUR EMOTIONS

It's wise to understand how emotions help you and how stifling them could hurt you.

Fear is our tricky fight-or-flight friend. If you ignore your fear, which is meant to protect you, you know the outcome if you've watched scary movies. Some of us enjoy thrillers because they teach us something, like how not to get killed.

Wisdom is the other gift when we're willing to dive into our fear—run toward the fire and write that book or fly on an overseas trip. But if we suppress or disengage from our fear, it has to go somewhere—down there, inside of us, until panic and paranoia rise and overwhelm our brains.

Loneliness is like a gentle friend; it tells us we deserve to reach in and reach out instead of isolating and feeling helpless.

Guilt and shame are highly connected. Shame is present, so we don't rob banks. Guilt reminds us we have values to uphold, like self-respect. Once we identify self-sabotage, guilt becomes the vehicle that transports us back to feeling good about ourselves, like not cheating at a card game.

When I win a round of cards with my husband, I celebrate because I won it honestly. I'm still working on not gloating. When I lose, I'm motivated to discover other strategies, which becomes a fun challenge.

When someone goes too far and shames us repeatedly, we get stuck in our sense of worthlessness. Guilt says we did something "bad," and shame tells us we *are* "bad."

As a reminder, one of the best ways to process shame and guilt is with an experienced counselor. You can learn to reclaim your values, make amends, and restore your true sense of self.

Even joy, if denied, can produce hysteria. I've met people who are afraid to be happy for fear it will be taken away. When you embrace that you are in charge and no one can take away your joy, hope and healing are your rewards.

This brings me back to my drumbeat: hating the narcissist only hurts us. Fear protects us by whispering into our ears that narcissists are master manipulators. Make friends with your fear, and you will learn that going no-contact is a very good idea.

WHAT YOU NEED TO KNOW ABOUT HATRED

Hatred has its pleasures. It is, therefore, often the compensation by which a frightened man reimburses himself for the miseries of fear.
The more he fears, the more he will hate.

~ C.S. Lewis

Hatred is the corrosive acid of the soul.

~ Unknown

History shows we're capable of doing horrific things to one another, and our current world climate is demonstrating that with increasing hostility. When healing from narcissistic abuse, it's crucial to work through anger and rage, yet it's imperative to address any tendencies toward hatred.

Many have used the h-word more than once when their anger blew past rage. Friends have told me they hate my mother for what she did to me. At the time I thought maybe I should hate her, too. She showed no remorse when I confronted her about my pain.

Hatred is a special kind of drug. When my friends said these things, I jumped into that pool of hate with them and splashed around in it. Other times, I felt cautious, knowing it was okay to dip my toe into hatred and experience one of the most intense human emotions, but just for a little while.

The late Karen L. Gold, Psy.D., wrote a brilliant article confirming this concept in the fall 2004 issue of *Paradigm* magazine, which is unfortunately no longer found online. She cites multiple research studies concluding that *hatred is highly pleasurable to the human brain.* People feel vindicated and righteous while in this intense state. It traps them in the past, fretting over events they cannot change, which can foster unrelenting insanity. Hatred also lures them into the future, plotting acts of joyous revenge, yet robs them of critically thinking their way out of it.

Since hatred is a debilitating and self-destructive emotion that feels good, it can become habitual, like an addiction. Think of hatred as an entity gone awry in your system. It's like the little narcissist inside you; it serves to annihilate your true self and absorb your identity to sustain its survival.

Did I hate my mother? No, but I thought I did. I now realize I hated being fearful of her, and that fear stifled my growth. If you've chosen to hate the narcissist who hurt you, remember that hating that person doesn't hurt them; it hurts you. Hate disguises insightful clues that the gift of anger teaches. Reconciling your fear and shifting into anger leads us away from addictive hate and offers us the fresh and proper perspective we need to move forward.

I learned that the best way to avoid the trappings of hate is to acknowledge your right to feel it but not to wallow in it. Verification from others that you've been wronged, plus self-validation, will help to calm your nervous system and help you return to your process of expressing anger.

Dr. Gold's research also found an unpleasant sensation even more intense than hatred and anger: extreme fear. C.S. Lewis astutely identified how fear and hate are intertwined. It seems logical to conclude that people who are triggered by fear-based ideology need truth-based affirmation from others to prevent hatred from spreading.

AN INSIDE LOOK INTO A NARCISSIST'S MIND

How do we release anger while still obsessed, shell-shocked, and confused by the injustice?

The answer arrived when I discovered a YouTube video by Professor Sam Vaknin from 2020.

His lecture on narcissism blew me away. It gave me a deeper understanding of the disorder than reading the *Diagnostic and Statistical Manual* (DSM) and helped me develop more empathy for those who suffer from NPD.

Vaknin reveals he was twice diagnosed as a malignant narcissist and argues that the best way to understand narcissism is by having a narcissist share his perspective on what it's like to be a narcissist.

I was mesmerized. Where did this guy come from? And how cool was it that he chose to share this information and give away the narcissist's game plan? My skepticism crept in, and I wondered if any of it was true.

When he insisted that implementing a no-contact cut-off with the narcissist is imperative, I was hooked again. I felt drawn in by his charisma, which was a bit unsettling, but finding him and learning this new, fascinating information was like discovering gold.

Vaknin says narcissists try to convince us they have all the power and we have nothing over them, but in reality, we have one hundred percent of the control.

He warned us not to be fooled. He described the mind of a narcissist as "a horror chamber, a concentration camp. There is no person there."

When I heard him say that, I was stunned. It took me a couple of days to process that one statement.

Vaknin reports that narcissists struggle with dissociation and have poor memories. They compensate for missing parts of data in their brain by maintaining false memories *without the intent of deception.* Therefore, people mistakenly accuse the narcissist of gaslighting!*

This was the validation I had been searching for. Childhood memories flooded my brain, and I questioned every scene. Was my mother going through the motions, pretending to love me?

Then I realized I was coveting the invisible ball of anger and repeatedly hurling it toward a wounded person I feared the most in my lifetime. I was perpetuating a spiraling shitstorm and would have continued had I not learned this truth.

It's vital to educate ourselves about the inner workings of narcissists and ditch the us versus them mentality. Narcissists are doing their best to navigate this world with

...

*Prof. Sam Vaknin, "Manipulate the Narcissist and Live to Tell About It? (Lecture in Budapest)," February 2020, 3:43:28. https://youtu.be/0uM13pZxBLM

a different kind of brain than we have. We have to learn how not to get caught up in their dynamics.

...

Sensitivity warning: If you choose to watch the video, please prepare yourself. It's a riveting yet challenging discussion. I summarize key points throughout the book.

Dr. Vaknin also has a collection of videos on his site: The Psychopathic Narcissist and His World Video Clips. https://samvak.tripod.com/narcissismvideos.html

PART THREE

Deprogramming

ABOUT DEPROGRAMMING

Are you living a life you want, or are you living a life you've been programmed? And the answer is, unfortunately, most of us are living a life we've been programmed.

~ Bruce Lipton

I remember being fascinated as a child watching a television special about a deprogramming intervention in an undisclosed hotel room. The intervention was for a young man who had joined a cult, and his heartbroken family was in attendance. Out of desperation, they lied to the man about the purpose of their meeting. Everyone took turns working with both the deprogrammer and the man, and it took three days for him to realize he'd been brainwashed.

Wow, my eight-year-old brain thought. I wanted to learn how to do that. Now I know why.

Deprogramming is a method of isolating individuals who've been brainwashed or coerced into joining a cult. The idea is to help them recognize that one or more individuals have been controlling them and they have the power to regain their independence.

It's not a cure-all intervention. Most cult intervention specialists use ethical, noncoercive techniques to counter the cult's unethical practices, and the person may become vulnerable again. It's essential to help them develop the skills and tools they need to protect themselves in the future.

Recovery time varies, as all situations are unique. In my case, it took me two years to fully comprehend the insanity of my situation and the loss of a mother-and-daughter relationship I thought was real. The first year, I experienced shock, denial, and rage. In the second year, I plunged into the spotlight before I was emotionally ready and authored a chapter in an anthology that hit the bestseller algorithm. Grateful for the support of my fellow authors, I found my courage. Lingering denial led to bargaining and, eventually, the last stage of grief, acceptance.

Fortunately, we have the advantage of healing on our terms and being as free as we wish, as long as we limit visits or go no-contact with the narcissist who started it all.

WHY IS THE HUMAN BRAIN SUSCEPTIBLE TO CULTS?

I've always wondered how cults brainwash people. For me, it was terrifying to know I'd been brainwashed from birth without a clue that it was happening or how to undo the damage.

Understanding the mechanics of cults can give us the confidence to avoid being deceived again. I was influenced by the cult of one, starting with my mother, to a professor, an attorney, and several boyfriends. Charmed by their bravado and my perception of their strength, they lured me in before I broke my cycle of vulnerability to narcissists.

We are all hardwired to bond with groups. Cult leaders often have intoxicating charisma and take advantage of anyone feeling lost, vulnerable, or isolated. They create confusion and cognitive dissonance within the targeted individual's mind.

Human beings are susceptible to cults for a variety of reasons. Some people are more vulnerable than others, but anyone can be at risk. Here are some of the main factors that can create susceptibility to cults:

- Ego-weakness and emotional vulnerability: People who are struggling with low self-esteem, anxiety, or depression are more likely to seek out a group that can provide them with support and validation. Cults often provide their members with a sense of community and purpose, which can attract people who feel lost or alone.

- Natural tendency to engage in dissociative states: People prone to daydreaming, fantasy, or trancelike conditions may be more likely to be drawn to cults that offer a sense of escape from reality.

- Weak, deteriorated, or nonexistent family relations and support systems: People who have experienced abuse, neglect, or rejection from their families may be more likely to seek out a cult that can provide them with a sense of belonging and acceptance.

- Depleted means of dealing with an urgent need for survival: People struggling to cope with the demands of everyday life may be more likely to seek out a cult that offers them promises of material success or spiritual enlightenment.

- History of severe child abuse or neglect: People who have been traumatized as children may be more vulnerable to cult recruitment because cults prey on their members' need for love and acceptance, which is appealing to those who experienced trauma or feel unlovable.*

...

*It's important to note that not everyone who might be vulnerable to cults will join one. However, the risk is higher for people with one or more of the abovementioned factors. If you are concerned that someone you know is involved in a cult or other group, you can contact the National Cult Hotline at 1-888-398-8225.

WHAT IF A NARCISSIST IS BRAINWASHING MY CHILD?

As of this writing, I have three friends who are heartbroken over their daughters' indoctrination by the cult of one. It could be a boyfriend, grandparent, or anyone who feels entitled to destroy the chance for family reconciliation.

If the parent exhibits narcissistic characteristics and is genuinely willing to seek psychotherapy to learn more about their behavior and origins, this could lead to a positive outcome for both parent and child.

There are other forms of brainwashing, such as *parental alienation*, in which one unstable parent, often the narcissist or the one with narcissistic traits, attempts to severely discredit the other parent in a false, negative light for the primary purpose of creating chaos and negative feelings within the child to damage the relationship with the other parent, who is usually the mentally healthy one.

A specialist or well-educated therapist can carefully guide the child or young adult toward a more stable and healing environment while creating distance from the one who initiates chaos. If the young adult is unwilling to go to therapy to resolve the problem, most likely due to fear of retribution by the unhealthy parent, the other parent is left wondering how to restore a connection with their child.

If your child's parent is a narcissist, you must work through third parties to resolve conflicts.

Reunification therapy is a family therapy specifically intended to reunite the child with a parent or parents with whom the bond has been broken. In the case of parental alienation, this therapy can be court-ordered. If the narcissistic parent is tasked to own up to their behaviors, therapy will probably not last more than one or two sessions. The most critical issue is the well-being of the child, and I do not recommend any therapy that gives the narcissistic parent a platform to create further damage.

Parents who are grieving the loss of their relationship with their child to a narcissistic partner or influential family member can seek out a counselor to help them build a stronger alliance with their child and learn strategies to help improve their child's mental health.

Sadly, some of these adult children do not reconcile with their parents. Some, not all, fall into the psychological trap of "taking one for the team," meaning they emulate the selfish family member and adopt and retain the role of the narcissist or one with narcissistic traits.

EIGHT STEPS TO LIBERATE YOURSELF FROM NARCISSISTIC INDOCTRINATION

Thankfully, those of us who embark on this journey have the power to heal on our own terms. We can liberate ourselves to the extent we desire until we are ready to take the inevitable, crucial step of going no-contact with the one who initiated it all.

The following is your template. There are no rules you won't understand and no coercion. Perhaps this book caught your attention because the name hit a nerve. You want to learn how to shed old stories, frameworks, and belief systems that are not inherent to your true nature.

1. *Accept this reality has occurred.* As weird as it sounds, the first step to healing is to acknowledge you've been abused. This can be difficult, as it means admitting that someone you loved and trusted has hurt you. But it's important to remember that you're not to blame for the abuse, and it's time to start de-

constructing lies you were told about yourself.

I remember saying to myself I had a mentally ill mother. Little did I know she had NPD. Although not liking this reality, accepting it helped me decipher all future revelations about her.

2. *Seek help and build a robust support system.* Encouragement from trusted helpers is vital and can come from various sources, including family, friends, therapists, and support groups. Going through this will evoke every stage of grief, but you won't be doing this alone.

I was fortunate to find helper-type friends who were willing to go above and beyond to get me through this. I felt broken but knew I desperately needed their attention and nurturing. Because of these special people, I healed my acute distress within five months. I still had moments of sadness, but it was nothing like before.

3. *Be patient with yourself.* Some days, you feel like you'll never recover. It takes time. There will be setbacks, but you can be grateful for how far you've come and keep going. You've got this!

4. *Focus on your own needs.* After being pressured by a narcissist to neglect yourself so you

could focus on them, it may take some time to get back into the habit of identifying what you need or want. It would be best if you made yourself a priority now, which means taking care of yourself physically, emotionally, and mentally. At first, this might feel odd or foreign, but push through that feeling. You'll eventually return to doing things that make you happy and feel good about yourself.

5. *Learn to love yourself* throughout the process (and after, of course!). One of the most important steps you can take after narcissistic abuse is to learn to love yourself. Accept yourself for who you are, flaws and all. Every step mentioned here is geared toward helping you do just that.

6. *Learn to Meditate.* Going within can help you become more aware of your true self and focus on your inner experience rather than focusing attention on others. Meditation is a lovely spiritual practice that can help you relax and de-stress. Research this topic and see what you gravitate toward. I recommend finding guided meditations on YouTube that appeal to you.

7. *Be able to identify the signs of narcissistic abuse.* There are many signs of narcissistic abuse, including constant criticism, name-calling, gas-

lighting, threats and intimidation, isolation and control, and unrealistic expectations. Again, there are multiple YouTube channels dedicated to teaching you about methods narcissists use to control others. Please educate yourself if you haven't done so already.

8. *Practice mindfulness*. Even now, I notice the tendency to pull back and push away in the way I was mistreated years ago. When that occurs, I return to my calming mantra, "I'm not a victim." In the moment, or maybe a few days later, I recognize that pushing people away in a hostile manner is not inherent to my true nature. Instead of giving in to old habits, I focus on gratitude that I caught myself before hurting another person, which was done to me repeatedly as a child. Mindfulness is the practice of being present in the moment. It can help you become more aware of and challenge your programming. I marvel at how far I've come, and it's possible to shed indoctrination like an uncomfortable wetsuit.

Deprogramming yourself is a process, but you'll get there faster than you think. Stay with it. Use your keen instincts honed from unstable relationships. Someday, you'll enjoy your life even more as you accept empathy in a symbiotic relationship.

Just don't rush it. An abusive boyfriend used to call me a "racehorse." I was depressed and wanted to hurry up and get life over with. I stayed in that relationship due to the familiar trauma bond, and I finally broke it off when his cruel behavior escalated.

During a recent moment of clarity, I realized I was playing out the victim role my mother wanted me to be in. I allowed myself to be hurt in these relationships.

It takes time and effort. Allow yourself to feel the pain and grief associated with severing it. It's okay to mourn the loss, even if it's a toxic relationship. You'll soon discover that changing your programming and finally living your desired life is attainable. Many people have been through narcissistic abuse and have come out on the other side.

I prefer to believe we never lose the essence of who we are. If we believe we have, then it could become a self-fulfilling prophecy, and we could stay lost or take longer to call our spirit back.

You are already the person you were meant to be; you just need to reclaim that part of yourself again. Maybe the narcissist experience was a temporary detour. What did you learn? That you already had all the power and were tricked into relinquishing a tiny bit? You are the master of your life, and you can create any scenario you wish. What we believe matters greatly. Believe then, perhaps, that this was a little hiccup. You are powerful, and through this experience, you learned how resilient you are when life presents challenges.

PART FOUR

Self Healing Strategies And Deprogramming Techniques

THE TREASURE HUNT FOR JEWELS OF AFFIRMATION

During the acute phase of grief, I needed something, a road map or some structure, to help me process this pain. I identified anxious behaviors and other traits I learned by remembering events, so I could proactively let go of reactions that were not authentic to my personality.

We can address these traits and let them go when we realize they are not a part of us. Emotional Freedom Technique, or tapping, helped me eradicate the emotion of jealousy I learned from my mother.

My mother and I were enmeshed, which means I didn't know where she began and I ended. My sense of self was unclear. I needed to separate from her and see us as individuals.

I journaled my actions, thoughts, and feelings as they popped up, trying to pinpoint exactly what I needed to eradicate from my life.

Instead of seeing this exercise as a chore or struggle, I turned it into a fun treasure hunt. This motivated my desire to unearth hidden jewels after sifting through the muck that encased them.

I encourage you to go on your treasure hunt.

To help you get started, here are some examples of excavated gems I found that provided valuable and insightful answers. Write each in either present or past tense, knowing that, no matter what, you are eager to overcome it all. I'm happy to report I no longer feel any of these statements.

- I am overly sensitive about not getting what I want.
- I become incredibly anxious when my husband goes to someone else's house without me.

  This triggered uncomfortable, intense, near-panicked feelings of abandonment without any factual reason. The confusion I felt helped me identify this was not my original pain.
- I feel overly concerned and hypervigilant regarding the well-being of others at the expense of my physical and mental health. I downplay my needs.

  I remember my true self being smothered and replaced with a false self, the one who was required to exist so I could survive my childhood.

- I feel overwhelming guilt.
- I don't feel good enough.
- I'm flawed in an irreparable way.

- I self-perpetuate shame cycles.

  I used to overreact to everyday situations in which I perceived my safety was acutely threatened. I would later feel terrible shame for my behavior. This was true of my experience growing up and not feeling physically or emotionally safe.

- I am afraid to put myself out there in the world.

  I was not allowed to shine, so I suppressed my talents. Hiding them became the norm.

  I received confusing messages: Show up, but don't steal your mother's spotlight.

  I stifled my expressive self in public but privately allowed my creative self to shine through cartooning, writing, and composing music.

- I was making life way more difficult than it needed to be.

  I believe my subconscious was attempting to keep me safe, so it tricked my brain into self-sabotage because it wasn't okay to be better than my mother. My handwriting is artistic, but it can be challenging to read. My mother's is impeccably near-perfect.

- I felt terrified my parent would brainwash my child against me.

  My parent instilled this fear when she spoke poorly about me to family members.

Looking over each one, I realized if my mother and I could've had a normal conversation, she'd tell me she felt most of these as well.

Last year, I wrote a cathartic, ten-minute play entitled *Are You...Really There?* about a mother and daughter in a fantasy scene where the daughter is able to fully express her anger and pain toward the mother, who responds kindly and helps her daughter through her grief. It was selected and performed at our city of Springfield's downtown theater, Hoogland Center for the Arts, and it was a life-changing event for me and others who told me it was their story, too.

This is why writing down your narcissistic parent's behaviors is valuable. Then, ask yourself, "Have I done that?" If so, "What steps can I take to change this behavior?" The answers will be clear.

Once I saw these gems, I transformed my treasures into positive intentions and truths:

Jewels of Affirmation

I have everything I need. I am happy and content.

I will never abandon myself.

I can care for myself and my needs before attending to others.

I forgive myself for not knowing how or what to do.

I am good enough.

I am not perfect, but I'm perfect just as I am.

I am safe in my home. I can peacefully resolve

conflicts.

It is okay to be seen. I can protect myself. I happily share my gifts when I am ready.

I can write legibly now and make my life easier in all ways.

I have a healthy, loving relationship with my daughter.

These all resonate as the truth to me now.

What comes to mind for you?

TAPPING WITH EFT

In 2008, I first learned about the Emotional Freedom Technique (EFT), or tapping, and incorporated this method into my practice. I graduated from feeling stressed and overly concerned about using the proper words to allowing clients to articulate their personal script as we tapped. The results of this method worked wonderfully, and I've been teaching it this way for the last sixteen years.*

EFT is a safe and effective method that's gradually gaining more acceptance in the medical field. When we tap on meridian points, we release negative emotions, thoughts, and feelings and are invited to replace them with positive

...

*For anyone who hasn't experienced EFT, please visit https://www.thetappingsolution.com.

They host a free Tapping World Summit every year around the end of February. I've enjoyed listening to presenters and learned volumes about the incredible healing scripts using this simple yet powerful technique. I encourage you to learn about the science of tapping and practice using it whenever you feel anxiety, fear, or any other uncomfortable emotion. You can process these states and feel calm and relaxed within minutes. I'm still amazed by the results.

ones. Not only does it provide immediate relief, but it also has a lasting effect.

One of my most profound tapping sessions occurred at age fifty. I tapped on the uncomfortable feeling of jealousy. I released sadness and pain about feeling left out. In my mind's eye, I saw my mother as a little girl in a bathing suit, holding her pet chicken. The youngest of three girls, she was tormented by the two older sisters who bullied and physically abused her. My mother might have adopted the victim role as a way to protect herself, as she did not feel safe in her home growing up.

I continued to tap. *Where was this going?*

And then, it was as if the room was filled with love. I felt compassion for my mother for the first time. Releasing anger through EFT allowed understanding to enter my heart and healed me in ways I never expected.

This insight allowed me to forgive her, which I wanted to do but didn't know how. At the time, I was still angry and feared if I forgave her, I would be vulnerable to her again. But I forgave her that day, and that feeling has remained since.

TAMING THE TRIGGERS

Discernment is the magic that releases us from the trigger.

~LKC

Because you've been toyed with by the narcissist, you will most likely get triggered by people who don't communicate in a way that conveys reassurance that "all is good" in the relationship.

That's why it's vital we understand how to lessen the frequency of triggers and absolve ourselves of the old curse of reactivity.

There are those who aren't deliberately trying to hurt you when they become bossy, unfair, or treat you unkindly. Most likely, they struggle with anxiety or depression and are having an off moment.

This is not easy for some of us to reconcile, especially if family members cannot be fully present in the way you need them to be. You desire a feeling of safety in the relationship. It's important to give them (and you) a bit of grace for everyone's benefit.

The problem remains: feeling disrespected and unsafe are two *huge* triggers for narcissistic abuse survivors. We get triggered because the narcissists in our lives didn't give a flying flip whether they were hurting us or not. We may escalate our anger energy from zero to one hundred again. It's important to recognize and remember the old dynamic is not actually happening. We do so by reminding ourselves we are safe and that these people are not deliberately trying to hurt us.

Trust me, you will know when you're being disrespected. Your body will cue you with a feeling of heat or whatever signal you recognize as "something's just not right." I can remember a time when I almost passed out from being yelled at by someone at work.

Most of us have learned when we focus on the positive, we receive a positive response, like a mirror. The same is true if we focus on the negative. If we react from that lower, energetic vibrational state, we get what feels like a tidal wave of repulsion coming back at us.

You will need time to focus your energy on the truth, not the trigger.

Give yourself a moment to breathe and realize you are overcoming all of this by not overreacting. Use the gift of observation and self-respect to cultivate the ability to demonstrate compassion for yourself and perhaps others at that moment.

And check in with yourself so you don't go into victim mode. The next time your emotional state accelerates from calm to intense stress in seconds, stop, take three big, deep breaths, and regroup. Train your brain to recognize that this moment of distress is not normal and you are no longer required to helplessly endure it. It only takes three breaths, amounting to thirty seconds of your time.

Have a go-to intervention in place to stop the pattern of overreacting and causing more harm when someone's energy is disrespectful toward you in any way.

To protect yourself, create "If I panic" notes on your phone or a document you can refer to. Read helpful phrases you previously wrote that will redirect you to snap out of it, like: You are safe, You are in control, You can handle this, You are not a target. Like a best friend on paper, you have already anticipated the situation. Instead of going into victim mode, which is easy to do because the narcissist taught you that by osmosis, take three deep breaths as you search for your phrases, which will help you regroup and restore your spirit that was previously scattered in several different directions.

You can also perform the tapping I discussed earlier, dance around while listening to your favorite music to expel pent-up energy, go out in nature, water the plants, or talk with a friend *after* you have calmed down.

My empathic husband has been the unfortunate recipient of one of my old habits: fast-talking, highly charged complaints about others. I have learned to reconcile those issues first and then talk with him. While it takes more effort, the payoff is feeling proud that you treated others with respect.

Focusing on the five senses can help us calm down. Perhaps you can visualize a peaceful scene. This could be a place you've been before or a place you've always wanted to go. Imagine the details of the scene, such as the colors, sounds, smells, textures, and tastes.

If you're like me and feel an abundance of negative energy in your body, hitting a bean bag with a soft bat is a great way to release intense emotions. If you imagine beating out the feeling of "disrespect," for example, you will release that out of your body. Make sure you don't scare people in your home with this method! Most people prefer EFT, I have been told because it feels less violent. I say: Great! Get it out any way you can.

When you finally relax, you can engage in meditation, a wonderful way to reconnect with yourself. Yoga is great for helping us release stored emotions in the body.

You can rise above your mind chatter when people are discourteous. You can also cultivate a circle of friends who are excellent communicators and respond within a decent amount of time, like a day or so. It's illogical to expect someone to reply right away unless they happen to be looking at their phone. It's nice to know the connection is there, and they honor you with a response.

Do your best to avoid stepping into the bitter hole, saying, "It's not fair! I have to sacrifice my feelings for theirs!" I've gone there in my head several times while dabbling with self-pity and victimhood. We don't always know everyone's story. We are all on this journey together of being born, living, and eventually dying. Compassion is the theme of this book, and the mirror of compassion will return to you.

Ultimately, you will allow people to be who they are without taking it personally. When you have done that, you will have conquered what was once thought impossible.

WRITE YOUR CUTOFF PROCLAMATION

It's only fitting we write a decree outing the kingdom of narcissistic maltreatment. It's your turn to have a voice now. This exercise will help you express everything you need to convey to a family member who will never acknowledge your words or value. This is similar to the empty chair technique, except you write whatever comes out. (Please note: This is a potent exercise, as you will see, and my recommendation is that you honor yourself and your journey by regularly seeing a therapist who can guide you through this.)

This doesn't have to be accurate or grammatically correct. Just let it fly and do its job.

Imagine your parent sitting across from you, unable to challenge your organic, free-flowing thoughts and words, which deserve to spill out and be heard.

I felt elated after writing mine. I proclaimed my freedom. My emotional state transformed from furious to joyful, from livid to loving. Like an exorcism on paper, I transferred a significant amount of angry energy from my body onto the page.

It was just for me. My words didn't hurt anyone, and I'll never show it to my parents. Even if, by chance, they did see it, I still have the right to express my feelings on paper.

I wrote my cutoff poem a few days after I allowed the realization about my mother to sink in. Sometimes, I would revisit my proclamation as a reminder of where and who I am in this process and also of how I must distance myself from her, knowing she'll never change. This realization was devastating, but I knew writing down my thoughts and feelings would be the best way to begin this crescendo of transformation on a page that doesn't talk back.

Write whatever you need to say. There is no right or wrong way. Just allow your most profound expressions to flow out.

Releasing my emotions on paper in a cutoff spew awakened me from the delusion I had failed as a daughter. This expression from my soul, my grand proclamation, freed me to see the truth.

Unfortunately, I was unprepared for the newfound sense of empowerment and the overwhelming grief that followed.

That's okay, I thought. I'm learning how to process emotions. I can be brave and keep going.

The reasoning in my proclamation about narcissism is inaccurate. That awareness came later. This exercise is only meant to help you purge on paper what you cannot say out loud to the parent who will never listen. Here is my cutoff proclamation:

You've been the most difficult person to
say goodbye to
because you're my mother.

I knew you from the first day of my life,
and we had extraordinary adventures together.
But you chose to embrace self-serving ways,
and you are a person I cannot be around.
Your toxic behavior and hateful way
you treat me—all of it is unacceptable.

Yet you delight in it.
You feel entitled to be cruel.
I have zero respect for you because you did
nothing to mentally improve yourself while
raising me.
Instead, you relentlessly blamed and shamed
this little girl until she broke.
Until she succumbed to your demands.
Until she took on your pain.

I have crawled out of the deep, dark, confusing
hole you placed me in, only to find myself in a
cage.

Yet, I had possession of the key all along, and I
found it, Mother,
I found the key to my freedom!
It burned in my hands as I unlocked my prison
because the pain of leaving this wretched exis-
tence that I once thought was love

> gave way to a new realization that I am living
> MY truth for the very first time.
>
> I now embrace ME and who I really am,
> with light and love all around me and
> those near and dear friendships I cultivated
> along the way.
> And I love myself, Mother.
> I love the person I am and the people I've chosen to be with.
> You cannot take me down. You cannot stomp
> on my spirit.
> I won't let you.
> There's nothing you have that I want.
> You have no power over me.
> This is over.
> I figured you out.

Writing this advanced my healing but also ignited suppressed rage. I could feel the vindictiveness she infused within me, pounding inside every vessel. A sick feeling rose in my throat as if needing to purge her out of my body.

I redirected this energy using EFT, and my physical symptoms subsided. Still, I felt an extreme need to be on the right side of the story. Even with all the tools in my nurse-therapist arsenal, I grappled with the unexpected intensity of this release. I was like an out-of-control locomotive, barreling down endless tracks without knowing how to stop the momentum.

And I was heading right back into that cage.

Again, my advice is: *Don't do this healing work alone.* I say this because it took years for me to finally stop neglecting myself. I was highly misguided to think that I could heal this alone with such bravado. When you know this emotional upheaval is more than you can handle, please reach out to a therapist who understands these dynamics, a narcissistic abuse support group, clergy, or a trusted friend for guidance and support. Most likely, you've already been through the worst earthquake. These are now aftershocks.

The overwhelming shame I felt when I overheard my mother complaining to others about me in our extended family wounded me for years. Her bad-mouthing affected my relationships with my cousins, who were already in their own predicament of shame from growing up with the multiple narcissists in our family. I had to resolve my tremendous fear that my extended family would reject me because they believed my mother's lies. I gave her so much power.

I found comfort with my husband and, surprisingly, my extended family, the people who I most needed confirmation and validation from. My cousins told me they never believed my mother and they were glad I cut her off. My heart melted. Several tons of anxious weight fell off my body.

Not long after that, I received an unexpected yet welcome phone call from my mother's older sister who was also my godmother. I was convinced she had believed my mother's lies for the past thirty years, so I never reached out to her. I was grateful she called to dispel that rumor.

"Your mother was always a brat and had a my-way-or-the-highway attitude," she told me.

Her words of confirmation gave me the closure I needed. She passed away a month later.

THE GREAT HAND SWIPE

My mother used to lie and gossip about me as if I were a petulant child, selfish to the core and obnoxious as hell. I believed it, so I was sensitive to the outside world's slightest criticisms. Yet somehow, I retained parts of myself because her actions confounded me. I knew I was a good kid with a corny sense of humor who cared about her friends and family.

Honing the skill of people-pleasing saved me from the looming brutality of my father at the direction of my mother. You can see why anyone who has been abused in this way would hang onto this coping mechanism throughout their lifetime. People-pleasing kept us safe in our scary households, so why not hang onto that coping mechanism as we venture out into the world?

I'll answer that: Because it's exhausting!

As an emerging adult, my anxiety would soar whenever someone spoke negatively about me. I didn't understand why I was so afraid of what others thought of me, even though it was clear from my past experiences. Unfortunately, my hyperfocused fear created a tremendous amount of stress which emotionally paralyzed my ability to reason and prevented me from finding any relief.

That's when it occurred to me that people-pleasing doesn't work in adulthood. There had to be another option.

One day, I raised my hand and swatted the air as if clearing a space to proclaim my new declaration:

I reject all definitions about me. From now on, I get to define who I am. No one else gets to.

I felt empowered. My inner child spoke these words, and I listened. I realized this meant that no matter what anyone said to or about me, it *didn't* matter—even compliments. People no longer had the power to define me on every level.

And it worked. When I was ready, I allowed myself to accept and take in positive comments again. Now, I enjoy a proper perspective of hearing sincere and kind messages from others and know when others are being disingenuous.

If a residual, haunting fear arises that people might speak poorly about me, I decide they don't know me, and I certainly wouldn't want to be associated with them. "I'm not that hard up for friends" is my mantra. I haven't needed to say that in a long time, but it's nice to know I can use it anytime, and it always reduces my anxiety.

I soon learned to incorporate phrases like, "No one gets to rain on my parade." And if fear of abandonment crept in like a ninja, I would shrug and tell myself, "They'd lose a great friend." It's remarkable how much you can build yourself up or tear yourself down with a simple thought.

Take back your power with one big hand swipe and create mantras or sayings to help you get to the other side. It's liberating! After a while, those mantras will be incorporated into your mind, and you won't have to remember to say them. They will become a part of you.

What hand swipe mottos inspire you the most?

SANITY SAVERS: GRATITUDE AND MANTRAS

Since narcissists never acknowledge the pain they've created (unless they attempt to fake it with love bombing), you cannot wait around for their apologies.

Gratitude will transform you into a mindset you may have never experienced before.

I spent way too much time obsessing over why my mother is who she is. And why it took me sixty years to remove her smoke and mirrors blindfold.

If you were brainwashed from birth like me, you can still become the best version of yourself. Start by writing your *gratitude list*. You know, your silver-lining statements.

Write down how you got through all of this unscathed. (Remember, you're not a victim.)

Ask yourself: What gratitude "I am" statements am I feeling right now?

Here are some personal examples:

> I am living a charmed life. Everything always works out for me.

I am grateful and receptive, I am fulfilling my life's dreams and desires, and I continue to allow all forms of abundance to come to me.

I am surrounded by kind, honest, and trusted friends and family who love and support me.

I am grateful I can travel knowing my daughter and son-in-law watch over my elderly parents.

I am free from dealing with my mother's unreasonable demands and games.

I am processing all challenges with love regarding my parents and will do it again when my parents are gone.

I am grateful for the beautiful lessons I learned from my parents.

You will find your life transforming into what you desire it to be. You can also use positive sayings to improve your health and manifest longevity. One of my favorite sayings is: Every day, in every way, I get better and better.

Being playful and imaginative are great ways to rekindle compassion in your heart. *Write down your "what ifs?"* Here are fun examples to illustrate how to use your imagination to create a new story about what could or might be happening on a spiritual level:

What if my parent tried to tell me what she needed, but I couldn't understand because I didn't know she had NPD?

What if my parent is sending me away so I can focus on myself?

> What if my parent had been in my life to show me contrast so I could know what I didn't want?
>
> What if all of this is a dream, and we will wake up on the other side where there is only love?

This entertaining way to expand your mind may help you to remember that we don't have all the answers, but we can imagine there's a reward for having traveled on this particular life journey, promising us renewed life, much like the flowers that emerge and bloom every spring.

TRANSFORMING ANGER INTO STRENGTH

You tell me, Don't shine in this world too brightly.
Your warnings make me hold onto my dreams so tightly.
~LKC

The narcissist tells you, "You can't launch a rocket." Your anger motivates you to build that rocket, and your inner rebel fuels it with the narcissist's negativity.

That rebel inside has saved us more times than we even know. If we overuse it to defy the narcissist, we can unintentionally undermine our success.

Instead of overreacting to the narcissist, focus your rebel anger toward cultivating your strength.

Your mind and body must release anger to initiate the cascade of stuck emotions from years of suppression. *I remind you to channel your anger through physical activity and creative means.* Heading outside for a brisk walk or run helps your body expel tension and improves sleep quality. And you never know what you might discover; I became a gifted sprinter after my daughter pulled me into road races. I had to be careful not to think about something I was angry about, or I would be running faster than my body could handle and hurt myself.

There are rewards for expressing anger or rage productively. As you know, I kicked a building with a flat foot. I'm surprised I retained my reasoning ability when my rage surged before I could process it. I've seen people hurt themselves doing this type of thing, and I wonder how much self-hatred had to do with it. But I digress.

I also expressed surges of anger through poems, art, and other self-soothing methods. EFT also worked wonders to release my anger and gave me a beneficial perspective to utilize this energy more. I may sound like I'm repeating myself regarding self-care, which I am because I'm encouraging you to use your inner rebel wisely instead of digging your heels in the ground. We are all climbing out of a cage we didn't ask to be shoved into. We are not victims. We are champions.

My beloved paternal grandfather was a cartoonist, and I discovered cartooning as another exciting way to express my emotional states as a child and into my adulthood, processing life events like a divorce. I would draw funny characters and entertain myself with stories. Later, I designed greeting cards, which were sold locally. It was my shared therapy, and people enjoyed the humor in my divorce cards and my distaste for bad boyfriends.

As a child, I yelled back at my mother because I naively thought if she knew how much pain I was in, she would stop. I'll never forget the brief conversation that forever silenced my efforts to communicate truthfully with her again.

"Mom, what you just said hurt my feelings."

"I don't care."

At age twenty, I wrote my first angry poem about her.

Since I couldn't reveal my pain to a narcissist, I poured everything out in writing. I validated my experience with every word, and it saved me from losing my mind. I recognized I was still vulnerable to her tactics, especially her love bombing, and there were times when the grief stages of denial and bargaining nearly swayed me back into the cage she so wanted to keep me in.

Writing led to composing music on piano and guitar. Growing up, my mother would respond positively, "That sounds good!" I enjoyed this method of expression and yearned for her approval since she was so difficult to please. At the time, I was unaware she was most likely feeding me praise to garner a "supply" for her empty void.

I found strength in expressing a part of myself that I had kept hidden. Doing so revealed talents I would never have discovered had my life been different.

MY FAVORITE F-WORD

Forgiveness is the fragrance the violet sheds on the heel that has crushed it.

~ Mark Twain

Besides *fun*, the other f-word I love is *forgiveness*. In the past, this word evoked a mix of trepidation and joy, especially when others insisted I'd experience a state of nirvana and I'd be missing out if I didn't embrace this cosmic gift.

I realize the value and power of forgiveness now. Like that ball of anger, we'll hang on to what's familiar as long as we need—until one day we surprise ourselves, lessen our grip, and let go of that energy. This opens our hearts to the possibility of allowing forgiveness to enter.

Forgiveness happens when we're ready. If a well-meaning person tells us we must forgive before we're prepared for that magic transformation, there's a chance we could go ballistic. It's a personal choice, and I honor where you are on this magnificent path to freedom. I challenge you to forgive others for pushing their timeline on you, and if they're open to learning, please share this concept.

Is forgiveness fun? That's for you to decide. I believe there's a sadness with forgiveness, a strange reluctance to let go of the hurt we enormously felt from a tumultuous ordeal. Did it mean anything for us to go through it, and why did we have this particular life experience? Does this action absolve the perpetrator if we let it go and forgive? Narcissists don't care whether you forgive them or not, so do it for yourself, so you can focus more on your recovery.

If we forgive our narcissistic parent, do we become vulnerable to their tactics? No. Does this fear prevent us from successfully healing our hearts and minds? No, because you'll eventually tackle fear since it's an unpleasant feeling. I was afraid to forgive my mother for fear that doing so would somehow weaken me, but I learned the opposite was true: I became determined and stronger in my convictions to move past a narcissistic-minded legacy. As we've learned, fear and hate are highly connected. Knowing this, I chose to find a way back to love, where everything makes sense.

I don't prescribe any particular religion, but one of my favorite quotes happens to be from Mother Teresa. It became my guiding light to the other side, to a world I didn't know could exist. She said, "I have found a paradox, that if you love until it hurts, there can be no more hurt, only more love."

ATTRACT HEALERS INTO YOUR LIFE

My mother always had a knack for intensifying my anxiety about the world. She used to walk around the house proclaiming she was going to animal heaven because people suck. I wouldn't even tell the bus driver my name on the first day of school because I was too afraid.

Since I had a lifetime of negative experiences with people, I didn't trust anyone. I thought I could figure all of this out myself. Why would I trust a mental health counselor—someone else who could toy with my mind? Years later, when I finally sought out a competent therapist, I learned to discriminate between the good people and the charlatans. What a relief!

And sometimes, life brings fantastic people into our lives. An unexpected encounter was in store for me when my husband and I went on vacation. That's when I met Barbara from the U.K. The moment we met, we immediately connected.

After returning to our respective countries, we kept in touch, pouring creativity into our texts and showcasing our mutual love for cartooning and its gift of facilitating the release of emotions. From across the pond, she spiritually held my hand and mothered me through my darkest times as I bravely questioned my mother's erratic behavior. Instead of defaulting into my usual, self-deprecating state, I paused to examine the truth emerging from a hidden part of my psyche, asking: What is fact and what is not?

My new friend helped me realize my mother doesn't have the capacity to care for me as I do for her. She offered what I call "positive thought spins" to lift me up, which reshaped my thinking and opened an inner dialogue about who I am. I trusted and surrendered. Barbara's love pulled me out and through to the other side, and today, our reciprocal bond is strong and unwavering.

This was a grand lesson in finding friends who reciprocate empathy. You might be tempted to reject them as old stories flood in, such as "I don't deserve this attention" or worse, "What if they're a covert narcissist?" Come along, and I'll help you with protective strategies to know the difference. And don't forget to pack your bravery.

PART FIVE

Beyond Grey Rock: New Protective Techniques

GO INTO YOUR SAFETY BUBBLE

When you fight monsters, you can become one.
If you don't go no-contact, you have to ask yourself why.
The human brain is very creative, and trauma bonding is as shape-shifting as the narcissist.

~ Dr. Sam Vaknin

Vaknin is correct in warning us about the perils of staying in a relationship with a narcissist.

He teaches us that narcissists want sacrificial victims, and I unknowingly fell right into my mother's trap.

Thankfully, I was aware of the Grey Rock method.

I can't help being slightly amused by Vaknin's claims of frustration for not being the one who created this highly endorsed technique. Grey Rock was coined by an American mental-health blogger named Skylar. It is a powerful tool for deflecting the narcissist's attention. The trick is to pretend to be one-dimensional and boring, offering no valuable information, which will irritate and confuse the narcissist, who eventually loses interest in you and retreats to find a juicier target.

My understanding of the Grey Rock method deepened when my mother asked about my financial status. Fearful of exposing certain parts of my life that needed to remain private, I withdrew, and my eyes glazed over.

"How much money do you have in the bank?"

"I don't know," I answered, looking away.

"What? You don't know your bank balance?"

"Not at the moment." I did my best attempt to look calm and unfazed.

"Well, that's stupid!" she muttered, hoping to shame me into submission.

With a nonchalant shrug, I signaled the end of the conversation. I knew I had emerged victorious because it was my first time shutting her down. The Grey Rock method empowered me to protect my boundaries.

As I've said before, I don't recommend toying with a narcissist, and Vaknin makes it clear not to do so. His message is that it doesn't matter how intelligent you are about narcissists; they are driven to accomplish what they do, as it is vital for their survival.

The more we understand about the way their mind works, the better we can respond if we find ourselves in an uncomfortable situation with a narcissist. I appreciate Vaknin's research and his willingness to educate us about the inner workings we've been ignorant of for centuries.

Even if we understand that going no-contact is inevitable, we need valuable skills to help us navigate while we grieve and plan our permanent exit from their lives. We're not light switches; we can't just turn off our feelings. It takes time to wrap our heads around the fact we just lost a parent to narcissism.

I offer strategies that can become arrows in your quiver

when you need them. They give us strength and reposition us as thrivers, not victims.

I developed the following narrative for a sensitive client who needed a way to exit an impossible situation with her family member. I shared this with several other clients, who encouraged me to include it in this book.

These words helped me on several occasions when I needed to remember I was no longer trapped.

> Create a safety bubble.
>
> Feel the greatest love imaginable surrounding you.
>
> When you do this, no one can hurt or define you.
>
> Politely excuse yourself if it becomes too much.
>
> You have the right to vacate a situation when you no longer feel appreciated.
>
> Stay calm and pleasant.
>
> Leave and say thank you.
>
> Be happy.
>
> Stay happy on the outside.
>
> Refrain from explaining yourself.
>
> Empower yourself by leaving.
>
> Show yourself that you can and will be peacefully assertive.
>
> Do it with grace, kindness, and love.
>
> There will be nothing to explain or feel ashamed about.
>
> You are merely taking care of yourself.

Stay in your healthy, healing, and safe bubble for as long as you need.

Experiencing a safety bubble can bring you peace and empowerment. Like Dorothy in the Wizard of Oz clicking her ruby slippers, this calming script reminds you that you're in charge and can always find your way home.

ACTIVATE YOUR SUPERPOWERS

Stop agreeing with others to be safe, I told myself.
You are safe within your incredible power.

~LKC

You have superpowers. You earned them during your experience. And you can activate them any time you like. For example, *confusion is a superpower.* There's a reason why things aren't making sense. Pay attention to why you're feeling confused, and journal about it. Just write and don't think. Let your intuition guide you. Soon, you'll have insights that will continue to help free you from your past.

It's like discovering you have a new arm extending from your back. It wasn't there before, but now you see it. You can easily scratch your back, knowing you have new superpowers and can implement them.

If you're interacting with the narcissist who raised you and you feel triggered, remember they taught you to feel this way. You're actively undoing their programming as you remind yourself of this. Stay present and be your own best friend, especially in this moment. Your determination for the truth will become stronger than your tendency to get caught up in memories.

Another superpower is your understanding that *you don't have to agree with others to stay safe.* You were unsafe in your childhood environment, but that's over now. Your superpower is knowing it's an old habit that you no longer need. So, stop agreeing with others to stay safe. You can remove yourself from the situation.

One of my favorite superpowers is to *be curious*. It's fun to rediscover the truth through curiosity. Imagine, like the ball of anger, there also exists a ball of shame. The quality I love most about curiosity is that it stealthily picks up the shame ball we no longer need and chucks it out the window so we can think more clearly about a situation. It's a relief to know we have this simple way of removing old dialogues from our heads.

After you begin this transformation, you'll develop the best superpower yet: an enhanced awareness, guided by your sensitivity, to recognize those who don't *feel* genuine. *Your heart is one of your wisest assets.*

I didn't know that a few years ago. My heart was energetically closed off inside a steel fortress. A friend gave me a gift certificate for a massage therapist because she knew I'd never spend money on myself. Before it expired, I scheduled an appointment. What happened next was profound. The therapist asked me to pretend to breathe through my heart.

"Um," I responded after an uncomfortably long pause on her table. "I don't know how to do that." I almost cried. Why don't I understand how the world works?

Her playful, angelic response calmed my anxiety and melted my shame. "That's okay. Put your hand over your heart and I'll put my hand over yours."

I wish I could tell you what she said next as I drew in a huge amount of air. I gasped, which startled me. It was as if I had to catch my breath after sobbing for hours.

"That's right," she coaxed. "There it is."

I felt tears rolling down both sides of my ears, dripping onto the blanket.

After the session, I texted my daughter, and I could feel my heart writing it. This gentle, gifted healer shifted something unknown yet incredible inside me.

Not long after that session, she announced she was moving to California. I nearly panicked, but I remembered that people are in our lives and then go on their separate journeys, and that's okay. My gratitude kicked in, and I realized she had given me a priceless gift before moving.

At her farewell party, I embraced her, choking back a million emotions, and said, "Thank you for opening my heart."

"*You* did it, " she said. I didn't believe her then, but she was right.

DOWN THE RIVER AND INTO THE CANOE

Unless you're ready for it, a cutoff can be abrupt and excruciating to handle. We can't just turn off love for our parents. And why would I want to shut down a part of me that loves? What would that do to my heart? I was already grappling with the loss of a relationship that was never based on reality. I needed my heart. And it wanted to help her.

I gave in to the bargaining stage of grief and revisited my childhood home. I spent time with my mother to see if there was any recourse. She was still that same, crabby old woman, except I knew her secret. I was also aware I could be seriously risking my mental health returning to that environment. I did my best to connect with my dad, hoping to salvage a relationship with the only parent I had left. My efforts to change my mother were futile. But I found a way to insulate myself from hearing her bully my dad and spew her lies in my direction.

How do we reenter this messy family dynamic, knowing who the narcissists are without succumbing to their manipulation? We can't help but feel nervous about ending up worse after we leave the situation.

That's when Down the River and into the Canoe came to me.

In the past, when my mother would make an awful comment to me, my heart would ache. Even with my energetic steel encasing it, I could feel her arrows of awfulness penetrating this precious part of me.

The next time I was around my mother, I didn't allow her arrows and barbs near my heart. Instead, I envisioned her comments rising into the air and floating over an imaginary abyss and down the river, away from me and into a canoe I saw in my mind's eye, where it contained and floated her bad thoughts farther away until they were gone. The river did all the work for me. I was shocked it worked and that I had protected my heart with my thoughts.

Because it worked, I began to have fun with it. Every time she would utter a bad comment, I would think, "There it is, and there it goes, down the river and into the canoe." I believed I had to be mindful and say this to myself as I imagined it happening every time.

But after a while, something very interesting happened. I no longer heard the bad comments. There she was, talking, but I didn't hear the words! It was as if my ears became selective—I developed selective hearing! This was unsettling for me, but shortly thereafter, I was relieved to hear her comments, yet this time they didn't hurt me. What was going on? Did I hypnotize myself to not let her words bother me anymore? Maybe I did, I thought. I had years of training in hypnosis.

Regarding grief, I had worked through my acceptance of her being a narcissist. On the other hand, I didn't like it, so I was bargaining. I wanted her to be normal. I even went further and thought, What if my love could save her? This was a very dangerous mindset, so this new technique helped me stay in a neutral place.

Once I realized she was never going to change, I solidified my acceptance. A vibration of peace and satisfaction flowed through my heart as if reflecting on the last sentence of a moving story.

Acceptance is very powerful. It helped me validate my situation. When one of her bad comments floated my way, I would tell myself, "Yes, of course, she would say that. That's what she does." The gift of acceptance is a blissful feeling that unfolds and envelops you. And this peace and kindness helps you make sense of what doesn't make sense. Why would somebody who cares about me say these critical things and be so cruel? Because they don't understand, because they are impaired in ways you cannot fix. And I have accepted that.

I have taught clients who have come through my door my canoe intervention. And they reported that they, too, no longer hear the bad comments in ways that hurt them.

Over the holidays, my mother said something critical to me once again. I remember hearing the comment but not making eye contact and happily moving on to a different subject. My terribly insecure mother no longer receives my wrath. What is there to get angry about? There's nothing else I can do but let it all go down the river, without even thinking about it now. She can't hurt me anymore.

THE MILLION DOLLAR QUESTION

Narcissists are like smoke and mirror magicians, skilled liars, and relentless manipulators. But the ability to generate your love is more powerful than any of these actions when you know their tricks. They've spent a lifetime honing these skills. What can be your advantage? For one, you're not mentally ill. Even if you feel like you haven't achieved a more normal state of mind, there's another thing you can do while you're on the mend. And that's asking the Million Dollar Question!

The concept is this: When you have a love interest or you're attracted to a new friend who seems exciting and fun, assume that person could be a narcissist and set protective boundaries until you're sure. It is always wise to allow time to help you determine if that person has NPD or narcissistic characteristics.

So, the Million Dollar Question you ask yourself is: "Is *that* person a narcissist?"

Ask anyone you trust who can give you an objective answer.

If you're not sure—and this is no joke—look up the

definition of a narcissist. Then, think about the person you're wondering about. Does he or she fit any of those descriptions?

If you're still not sure, ask a trusted friend.

I casually asked a friend one day if someone we both knew was a narcissist. "Oh yeah," he said emphatically. "He's definitely a narcissist." I was shocked I hadn't picked up on that, but I was grateful for his feedback. I asked how he determined that and what behaviors he noticed so I could use this in the future. Thinking back, I had always known but didn't want to admit it. When I accepted this and verified my friend's observations, it was irrefutable.

If a new person comes into your life, and you find yourself gravitating toward that person, take a step back and ask, Is this too good to be true? Is this person needing something from me that I don't want to give away, like my personal power? What's really in it for them? Be persistent. Again, ask a trusted friend, or read the definition of a narcissist. Use yet another one of your superpowers—empathy—to see if that person fits into that definition and allow a crystal clear answer to come through.

THE PRO AND CON EXERCISE

This simple method will give you the confidence to make good choices regarding who you allow into your inner circle before you lose perspective. This is especially helpful when you are dating.

I used this to determine whether or not I wanted to continue seeing this new guy I met at a wine tasting. I realized all his great qualities outweighed some of the downsides I picked up about his personality. I did the Pro and Con Exercise, and I've been happily married to him for the last twenty-four years.

Draw a line down a sheet of paper. Write Pro on one side and Con on the other. On the Pro side, list what you like, the positives, how you feel, etc. Do the same on the Con side. What did this person do that made you pause and go "Uh-oh." Don't overthink; write. After you're done, see if any of the characteristics on the Con side is a deal-breaker. If so, it's better to know now. If the Pro side outweighs the Con side, meaning if you generated an extensive list of great things you liked about the person and you can handle minuscule items on the Con side, then keep dating and be watchful.

While you're learning this skill of discernment, it still doesn't hurt to check in with trusted friends if you're not sure. You will ultimately make informed, good decisions about who is right for you.

WHEN THE NARCISSIST SCREWS UP

Narcissists can get caught in their own webs once in a while. They will make a big mistake and attempt to blame you. When this situation lands in your lap, run! Use their poor behavior to your advantage, make it clear they permanently messed up, and exit the scene. It's a gift!

When narcissists fall into their own hole and scramble to get out, these are opportune moments. Yet, depending on where you are in your process, we sometimes aren't ready to let them go, or worse, we give them a pass. I've done it. Don't worry if you miss your chance to leave the relationship while pointing a finger at them. They'll do it again, and you'll be ready next time.

Remember, you have the right and complete control to cut off narcissists whenever you wish. You don't have to wait until they do something egregious.

If your mission is to connect with other family members before cutting off narcissists in the family, you can give yourself a *short* time window to do that, but please, always use protective techniques. The best one is remembering you can leave any time you wish no matter how hard they try to shame you for doing so. They'll shame you if you stay, so really, what's the difference? Do it. Honor yourself. You are no longer tethered to them or your childhood home.

These opportunities come and go, and narcissists act like nothing happened. As we now understand, this is because they have terrible memories. They are not necessarily attempting to gaslight you; they don't remember the big bad thing you are accusing them of. They'll act like there's nothing to see here.

Unfortunately, conditioned partners see the opening but are often too invested in the relationship and have a solid trauma bond, so they are less likely to flee.

My dad's life depicts this quite well. Being four years older than my mother, I think he's trying to outlive her. I have a handful of friends cheering him on. It's fun meeting him in the grocery store and listening to him complain about how her list doesn't contain items he needs. He's coming around, I think. He knows she's not a nice person, yet he can't wrap his head around the indisputable fact she's a narcissist. But he always surprises me. When we were picking out sweet potatoes, he asked me to help him find the medium ones because she's so particular and he fears her wrath if they aren't the right size. "She makes things difficult" will fly out of his mouth and make me chuckle. He gets it. Even better, he knows she's lying about me. I'm not the distant, manipulative, selfish daughter she wants him to think I am.

Returning to that house to reconnect with my dad was worth it.

Even when you *do* catch narcissists in the act of undeniable folly, they will negate it and quickly turn it around and blame it on you, or they'll attempt a love bombing to entice you back. For example, when the healthier partner files for divorce, the narcissist decides to feign normalcy for a week. When the partner catches on that it's all an act; the narcissist shifts back into old habits, such as the silent treatment. Narcissists will deny they are doing this, which reinforces the partner's decision to exit the relationship.

CONCLUSION

SAYING GOODBYE TO FAMILY ENABLERS

To those who believe you can maintain relationships with enablers, please understand your efforts to reverse years of indoctrination by the family narcissist will fall short. I didn't want to accept this, but it's the truth. I learned how to reclaim my life after relinquishing it to the family narcissist. I had complete control over that part of my life.

However, I wasn't ready to face the reality that my dad would eventually bend to the family narcissist's whims at the cost of losing his daughter. In graduate school, I studied emotional abuse and learned that the conditioned human mind will comply with any demands from the aggressor to escape beratement. Knowing this helped me understand the dynamic in our family, but it didn't release my pain.

When my father reached out to me after I cut off my mother, I agreed to meet him without her around. When that happened, I felt like I had won a trophy. My dad, the man I've always needed to pay attention to me, called me out of the blue, and there we were, having lunch, and no one was contaminating our conversation. I don't regret one second of this opportunity to feel what it was like to have a normal relationship with a parent. That was the last gift he ever gave to me.

In our moments together, I felt loved and cared for. I asked him questions I had longed to know the answers to. Part of me knew this time with him would be short-lived, as I focused on his advancing age, not his consuming guilt brewing inside. I relished my experience of having my dad all to myself. He was kind and occasionally expressed sadness and confusion about being "caught in the middle." Yet he met with me once a month anyway.

I invited my husband to join us for lunch, and my dad was thrilled. After a fantastic visit, my dad ended our welcome respite from the family narcissist by announcing from across the table, "I will tell her I did this today with you."

It was nice while it lasted. I sat there in shock while his blissful ignorance permeated the room.

The little girl who remembered being vulnerable to my mother resurfaced with a dread I hadn't felt in years. I heard myself bargaining while he gleefully signed the check as if creating a paper trail for my mother was his proclamation to unite our family again. He was so consumed with pride in his new role as a peacemaker that I'm not sure he even heard me.

"Then be ready to say goodbye to these outings and our time together," I warned, bordering on disrespect. In the parking lot, I pleaded again, feeling defeated as intense shame enveloped me like an unwelcome hug. I watched his eyes glaze over.

After feeling dejected all weekend, I had to remind myself that I already received what I needed from him: to know

I wasn't crazy and that at least one of my parents loved me. But I wasn't ready to say goodbye to our sacred time together, and my fury over this ordeal escalated. No amount of running, walking, or meditating helped that day, which terrified me. I even considered drinking alcohol again and stopped short of uncorking a bottle of wine, realizing I was self-destructing. Over who? Over what? It was over.

Once again, I had allowed myself to be the recipient of someone else's crucial decision. My dad was clueless that the puppet strings my mother used to control him reached the restaurant that day. Even I didn't want to admit it, but it was true: I had to limit my time with him if he was going to jeopardize my mental health. I learned that we must eventually say goodbye to family enablers. Other family members will tell me to keep my options open, but why would I expose myself to this future predictable chaos?

I had to make my own decisions and not allow others in the family or anyone else to influence me. It was time to move on, and now I had to grieve the loss of my dad. He couldn't awaken to the truth that his sacrificial service to the family narcissist ruins relationships. While I didn't feel manipulated by him, I knew his role to indoctrinate me was coming. This new gift of wisdom helped me realize that I can't be around her to appease my dad.

I still felt anger rolling around in my body, which motivated me to craft a letter to him. I thought if I could reprogram him to help him understand his wife is a narcissist, yet not say the dreaded word, he'll finally understand. "She is who she is" is the closest phrase we agreed upon. But then I realized I was fighting with no one except myself. I ripped up the two-page letter.

This ended my lifelong sentence of chasing after unavailable people. Gratitude brought me back to reality. Maybe I was delusional, but not entirely. I felt his love. And then, he morphed back into an enabling servant and was gone.

Lies shackle us in captivity. I may feel sadness about this truth regarding my parents, but grieving this new loss will pave my way to freedom.

The hardest part is when we see those glimmers of hope. We reach out for them, forgetting an unspeakable betrayal awaits our experience.

For me, the price of searching for love inside a confined parent was worth the heartbreak. We have to process the loss and go through it anyway, so why not find out if there's a spark of love still left in the emotionally hijacked parent? We're not misguided in this endeavor; we want to see if it's really there. And if not, we can retreat into ourselves for safety and love. We can make better choices by connecting with those who enhance our lives and don't challenge our worth. And that's the lesson. To rise above adversity and find ourselves again.

RANDOM THOUGHTS ABOUT THIS SILVER LINING

I woke up from a vivid dream. I was a child crawling out of the mud and saw my adult self. My child looked up and said to my adult: Now you get to be you.

~LKC

We all grieve in different ways. When memories come up, give yourself the attention you deserve. Most days, you will focus on them as valuable insights. On other days, you might linger in the confusion you once felt. It's all part of the grieving process. Please be patient with yourself.

You are now part of a special group of people who figured out the narcissist's game. So many of us have bravely scrutinized our actions and broken narcissistic patterns within ourselves and lessened any chance of them permeating into our precious young family members. Our descendants will benefit from our challenging journey. We can only hope they won't have to endure the same trauma or feel the sting of the narcissist's whip in words and actions. Perhaps we are better prepared to teach them how to show compassion for bullies while maintaining good boundaries.

We freed ourselves because we dared to admit the unthinkable. It's mind-bending to think the people we expected to love us instead cursed us for being ourselves, yet we defied them all.

Our new understanding of the narcissist's true character and inner experience allows us to make choices as we set solid boundaries. We can let go, plan our new life and continue to nurture our compassionate hearts.

Would I trade my narcissistic parent for a nonnarcissistic one? While I admit to fantasizing about what my life could have been if I had different parents, I wouldn't change my life experience. Like a card game, you play with the hand you're dealt. For most of my life, I had become a shadow of a narcissist to survive. I discarded the false self I needed to stay safe and recovered the essence of my true personality.

I credit my childhood self for finding solace with her dog, writing in her diary, composing music, and creating art. Later in life, I was fortunate to experience incredible love from my husband, amazing in-laws, and their children and families. They helped me see what love really looked like.

My friend in the U.K. reminds me, "If you had nothing to climb out of, life would be so boring!" She's right. I've come a long way since then. I don't dislike narcissists I've met in my lifetime or the ones I'll meet in the future. I now see them for who they are: People trying to make sense of this world. They have no magic powers over us, although they strive to convince us otherwise.

I wonder what kind of world we might have if we all understood the way narcissists think. We'd set boundaries to resolve encounters with them more peacefully, I imagine.

My sadness for them expanded my heart. I overcame

abuse by turning inward and found a love inside of me I never knew existed. I can now tap into all aspects of my creative soul, and every day is another beautiful chance to surprise myself with spontaneous expressions of the true me. I finally get to know her now.

WRITE FROM THE HEART: YOUR THANK YOU AND GOODBYE LETTER

My life would have been different had I not experienced my mother's narcissism, but here I am. What am I going to do about it? Did I go through this for nothing? Hell no, I didn't! I'm writing my thank you letter so I can get on with my best life.

~LKC

Expressing gratitude for what we've been through seems like a tall order, but it's one of the most unexpected ways I felt complete again. I allowed my heart to shine, and that felt amazing. I discarded the remaining bitter parts of myself that I didn't know I was still carrying.

Writing a heartfelt Thank You and Goodbye Letter to my mother became an exercise that helped me express my love. In doing so, I found my boundary of done. I share my successes as if she were able to respond appropriately had she not had a mental illness.

My mother will never receive this letter because I wrote it for me.

If you're ready, I invite you to write your heartfelt letter to the family member you lost because of NPD. My hope is you will feel free and empowered, with a lingering sense of bliss.

If this doesn't feel like the right timing, please honor where you are in your journey. I'd like to reassure you that you're exactly where you need to be at this very moment. You can always come back to this later.

Either way, I'm rooting for you!

Here is my Heartfelt Thank You and Goodbye Letter:

Dear Mom,

I forgive you.

You didn't ruin my life.

I am a happy, successful, and joyous person.

It was most gratifying to rise from the ashes like the phoenix.

I have thought about your history, Mom, and I know it wasn't easy growing up.

I do miss you and all the good things you did for me.

I love you and wish you the best in your final years.

Linda

ENCOURAGING WORDS

My boundaries are more solid than they used to be. I trust myself. I am better, not perfect, at identifying narcissists. It took me years, but I was determined, and I continue to use my own strategies to guide me. As I awaken to more insights about myself, I gain confidence in my ability to tap into my heart and direct my path. You will attract more like-minded angels in the world who will ignite your lovely heart to spread these messages.

I learned to overcome perfection when I knew it was unattainable. When residual shame flares up, I tell myself, "You get to be human." This reminds me that I can make mistakes like everyone else and admit to them without feeling ashamed. And if anyone attempts to shame me for my mistakes, I will see that it's not me who needs reevaluation.

Blaming was a trait I learned from my mother, and I love that I could unravel sixty years of entangled indoctrination so quickly. And everyone's different. There's no right or wrong amount of time to heal. But I'm willing to bet you're just as determined as I was to figure it out and get on with your life—your real and true life of freedom.

You have the tools to finish the work within yourself, and I'm glad we healed in this journey together. My goal was always to share valuable information for your expansion and growth, dear reader. Finishing this book ended a significant amount of sadness and pain and gave me renewed freedom in this life.

I'm no longer afraid of narcissists because I understand them now. My deepest wish is that you do, too.

ABOUT THE AUTHOR

LINDA K. CASTOR is a registered nurse and psychotherapist in private practice. Her Master's thesis, *Subtle Cruelty: Emotional Abuse*, was well received at The University of Illinois at Springfield, where she graduated with honors. She wrote a wellness and mental health column for the *State Journal-Register*, Living Smart with Linda Castor (2012). She is a contributing author in *Shaman Heart Sacred Rebel* (2023). Linda enjoys traveling with her husband and is an accomplished sailor. Learn more about Linda at https://lindacastor.com.

Made in United States
Troutdale, OR
05/04/2024

19642073R00076